D1242715

BIG-TIME RECORDS

BIG-TIME
BASEBALL RECORDS

BY BRUCE BERGLUND

CAPSTONE PRESS
a capstone imprint

Published by Capstone Press, an imprint of Capstone.
1710 Roe Crest Drive
North Mankato, Minnesota 56003
capstonepub.com

Copyright © 2021 by Capstone. All rights reserved. No part of this publication may be reproduced in whole or in part, or stored in a retrieval system, or transmitted in any form or by any means, electronic, mechanical, photocopying, recording, or otherwise, without written permission of the publisher.

SPORTS ILLUSTRATED KIDS is a trademark of ABG-SI LLC. Used with permission.

Library of Congress Cataloging-in-Publication Data
Names: Berglund, Bruce R., author.
Title: Big-time baseball records / by Bruce Berglund.
Description: North Mankato, Minnesota : Capstone Press, 2022. | Series: Sports illustrated kids big-time records | Includes bibliographical references and index. | Audience: Ages 8–11 | Audience: Grades 4–6
Identifiers: LCCN 2021004146 (print) | LCCN 2021004147 (ebook) | ISBN 9781496695451 (hardcover) | ISBN 9781977159304 (paperback) | ISBN 9781977158901 (ebook PDF)
Subjects: LCSH: Baseball—Records—Juvenile literature.
Classification: LCC GV867.5 .B47 2022 (print) | LCC GV867.5 (ebook) | DDC 796.357—dc23
LC record available at https://lccn.loc.gov/2021004146
LC ebook record available at https://lccn.loc.gov/2021004147

Summary: Few things beat the drama of a player smacking a big home run at the ballpark—except when that big homer sets a new record! Behind every big-time baseball record is a dramatic story of how a player or team achieved greatness on the field. With legendary players at the plate, on the mound, and in the field, here are the record-setting moments that will keep baseball fans turning the page for more.

Editorial Credits
Editor, Aaron Sautter; Designer, Sarah Bennett; Media Researcher, Morgan Walters; Production Specialist, Laura Manthe

Image Credits
Dreamstime: Jerry Coli, spread 36-37; Getty Images: George Rinhart, 22, George Silk, 21, Louis DeLuca, 19, Transcendental Graphics, 6; Library of Congress/Bain Collection/ Prints & Photographs Division, 25, 52; Newscom: AARON JOSEFCZYK/UPI, 48, AFLO, 41, Dick Druckman/ZUMA Press, 5, Frank Jansky/Icon Sportswire DCT, top 33, GARY HERSHORN/REUTERS, 43, Peter Joneleit/Cal Sport Media, 27, PHIL MASTURZO/TNS, bottom 33, Rob Tringali/SportsChrome, 47, UPI/Kevin Dietsch, Cover, USA Today Sports/ Kim Klement, 17; Shutterstock: bioraven, bottom 42, Dolimac, 12, J.D.S, 29, lazyintrovert, top 42, Michal Sanca, 20, Puwadol Jaturawutthichai, (flags) 49; Sports Illustrated: Al Tielemans, 23, Damian Strohmeyer, 39, David E. Klutho, 7, 13, bottom 28, 35, Erick W. Rasco, 14, 16, 53, Heinz Kluetmeier, 51, John Biever, top 28, John Iacono, 54, Mark Kauffman, 59, Neil Leifer, 31, 45, 57, Robert Beck, 8, 9, 10, 11, 24, 30, 34, V.J. Lovero, 44

All records and statistics in this book are current through the 2020 season.

Printed and bound in the United States of America. PO4270

TABLE OF CONTENTS

WORDS IN **BOLD** APPEAR IN THE GLOSSARY.

AMAZING BASEBALL RECORDS

Fans were ready for history to be made on September 28, 2019. More than 32,000 people filled Citi Field, home of the New York Mets. Every time first baseman Pete Alonso stepped up to home plate, the fans took out their phones and cameras. They wanted to capture a major moment in baseball history.

The night before, Alonso had hit his 52nd home run of the season. This tied the Major League Baseball (MLB) record for most home runs in a season by a **rookie**. There were only two games left in the season. Would he get one more homer to break the record?

Alonso struck out in his first at-bat. In the third inning, he came to the plate again. The pitcher threw two balls and one strike. Then he threw a fastball, and Alonso crushed it. As the ball flew high over the centerfield fence, fans jumped to their feet and roared. Alonso had 53 home runs for the season—the most ever hit by a rookie.

> The record that Pete Alonso broke wasn't very old. Just two seasons earlier, New York Yankees centerfielder Aaron Judge had hit 52 home runs as a rookie in 2017.

Pete Alonso celebrated after hitting his record-setting home run against the Atlanta Braves on September 28, 2019.

Most Home Runs by a Rookie, Season

RANK	PLAYER	TEAM	SEASON	HOME RUNS
1	Pete Alonso	New York Mets	2019	53
2	Aaron Judge	New York Yankees	2017	52
3	Mark McGwire	Oakland Athletics	1987	49
4	Cody Bellinger	Los Angeles Dodgers	2017	39
5	Wally Berger	Boston Red Sox	1930	38
5	Frank Robinson	Cincinnati Reds	1956	38

Some baseball records last a short time. But others have lasted for decades. Baseball is an old sport. Fans have been cheering for their favorite teams for more than 140 years. The National League (NL) started in 1876, when people were still riding in horse-drawn carriages. The American League (AL) began in 1901.

Baseball was very different back then. Pitchers played in a lot more games, and they usually pitched entire games. In 1884 Charles Radbourn pitched an incredible 678 innings for the Providence Grays in Rhode Island. He won 60 games that year—the all-time record in baseball. Today's pitchers don't come close to Radbourn's performance. In 2019 the best pitcher in baseball was Justin Verlander. He won 21 games and finished with 223 innings pitched.

Baseball has changed over the years. Some old-time records will never be broken. But a few modern players, like Aaron Judge, Pete Alonso, and Justin Verlander, are bigger and stronger than many players in the 1800s. They can hit the ball farther and throw the ball faster. Today's players set amazing new records every year.

Charles Radbourn played for five major league teams, including the Providence Grays and the Boston Beaneaters.

In 2011 Justin Verlander won both the Cy Young and Most Valuable Player (MVP) awards for the American League.

Radbourn vs. Verlander

Charles Radbourn, Providence Grays, 1884

Team's total games: 112

Games Radbourn pitched: 75

Games Radbourn won: 60

Justin Verlander, Houston Astros, 2019

Team's total games: 162

Games Verlander pitched: 34

Games Verlander won: 21

BIG-TIME HITTERS

Hit Master

One of the longest-lasting records in baseball was the mark for most hits in a season. In 1920, George Sisler of the St. Louis Browns had 257 hits. For the next 80 years, no player had more than 240 hits in a season. Sisler's record looked like it would never be broken.

Then in 2001, an exciting player from Japan entered the league. He was called a rookie, but Ichiro Suzuki had already played nine seasons of pro ball in his home country. He won three straight MVP awards in Japan and was famous across the country. Everyone called him "Ichiro."

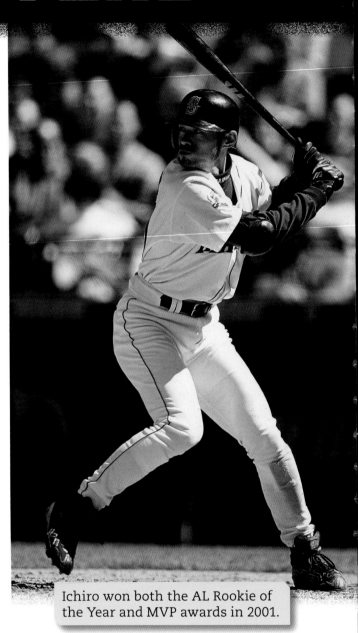

Ichiro won both the AL Rookie of the Year and MVP awards in 2001.

In his first season with the Seattle Mariners, Ichiro had 242 hits. Then in 2004 Ichiro broke George Sisler's record with 262 hits in a season. When he retired in 2019, he had a combined total of 4,367 hits in the U.S. and Japan—the most ever by a pro baseball player.

MOST MLB CAREER HITS

RANK	PLAYER	SEASONS PLAYED	TOTAL HITS
1	Pete Rose	1963–1986	4,256
2	Ty Cobb	1905–1928	4,189
3	Hank Aaron	1954–1976	3,771
4	Stan Musial	1941–1963	3,630
5	Tris Speaker	1907–1928	3,514

In 2020, Albert Pujols had the most career hits of any active player. At the end of the season, he had 3,236 hits.

Youngest Cycle Hitter

From his first full season in 2012, Mike Trout showed that he was going to be one of the best players in the MLB. He won the 2012 AL Rookie of the Year award and came in second for the MVP award.

Trout has become one of the best all-around players in the game. He excels at drawing walks, running the bases, hitting home runs, and playing centerfield.

Trout also set one notable record. He's the youngest American League player ever to hit for the cycle. A player gets the cycle when he hits a single, double, triple, and homer in the same game. Trout did just that on May 21, 2013, when he was just 21 years old.

The youngest player to ever hit for the cycle was Mel Ott. He was just 20 years old when he did it with the New York Giants in 1929. More than 300 players have hit for the cycle in the history of baseball. But Mike Trout was one of the youngest ever to achieve this amazing feat. Every year, he is among the best players in the league.

In a game against the Cincinnati Reds in 2018, Milwaukee Brewers outfielder Christian Yelich had a rare achievement. He became only the third player since 1900 to hit for the cycle twice in the same season. But his feat that day was **unique**. He is the first to hit for the cycle twice in the same season—against the same team.

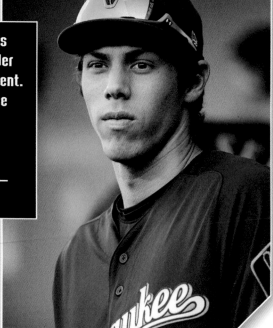

Mike Trout won the AL MVP award three times in his first eight seasons.

Baseball's Hardest Hitter

Baseball fans love following their favorite teams and players. Hardcore fans especially love newfound records that track just how good their favorite players really are.

One method uses **radar** to measure how fast a ball moves after a batter hits it. The ball's speed when coming off the bat is called its exit **velocity**. To get good exit velocity, a player needs to be strong, and he has to swing the bat fast.

Baseball's hardest hitter is Yankees outfielder Giancarlo Stanton. Since MLB began keeping exit velocity records in 2015, Stanton has had the fastest hit every year. Balls have left his bat moving faster than 120 miles (193 kilometers) per hour.

HOW FAST IS 120 MILES PER HOUR?
Fastest sprinter, 27 mph (43.5 kph)
Average speed limit on highways, 70 mph (112.7 kph)
Cheetah, 75 mph (121 kph)
Wind speed in a F1 tornado, 112 mph (180 kph)
Giancarlo Stanton's fastest hit, *123.9 mph (199 kph)*
Golden eagle, 199 mph (320 kph)
Racecar, 240 mph (386 kph)

Stanton's hardest hit came when he played with the Miami Marlins. It had an exit velocity of 123.9 mph (199 kph), but it didn't count as a hit. The ball flew right to the second baseman for an out.

The Bomba Squad

In 2018 the Yankees set a new record for most total home runs in a season with 267. Their lineup featured two of baseball's most powerful sluggers in Giancarlo Stanton and Aaron Judge. In 2019 it looked like the team would break its own mark by hitting more than 300 homers.

But the Minnesota Twins were having an incredible season of their own. The Twins didn't have big-name superstars like Stanton and Judge. Their best-known hitter was six-time All Star Nelson Cruz. The other Twins players were young and not well known—but they could all hit homers. Eight Twins players each hit more than 20 home runs in 2019.

Going into the last day of the season, the Twins were behind the Yankees in total home runs. Aaron Judge slammed a home run for the Yankees, giving them 306 for the season. But three Twins went deep in their last game, giving the team the new season record with 307 homers.

Nelson Cruz led the 2019 Twins with 41 home runs.

The 2019 Twins had several players from Latin America on the team. They used the Spanish word *bomba* for home runs. They liked to call themselves "The Bomba Squad."

Most Team Home Runs in a Season

RANK	TEAM	SEASON	HOME RUNS
1	Minnesota Twins	2019	307
2	New York Yankees	2019	306
3	Houston Astros	2019	288
4	Los Angeles Dodgers	2019	279
5	New York Yankees	2018	267

Most Player Home Runs in a Season

RANK	PLAYER	TEAM	SEASON	HOME RUNS
1	Barry Bonds	San Francisco Giants	2001	73
2	Mark McGwire	St. Louis Cardinals	1998	70
3	Sammy Sosa	Chicago Cubs	1998	66
4	Mark McGwire	St. Louis Cardinals	1999	65
5	Sammy Sosa	Chicago Cubs	2001	64
6	Sammy Sosa	Chicago Cubs	1999	63
7	Roger Maris	New York Yankees	1961	61
8	Babe Ruth	New York Yankees	1927	60
9 (tie)	Babe Ruth	New York Yankees	1921	59
9 (tie)	Giancarlo Stanton	Miami Marlins	2017	59

BIG-TIME PITCHERS

Baseball's Fastest Flamethrower

Radar is useful for more than seeing how fast a baseball is hit. Coaches and **scouts** also use it to find out how fast a pitcher can throw a ball. Most MLB pitchers can throw over 90 mph (145 kph). A few pitchers can even throw faster than 100 mph (161 kph). These players are sometimes called "flamethrowers."

Today's fastest flamethrower wasn't even a regular pitcher on his high school team. Jordan Hicks usually played outfield. But since starting with the St. Louis Cardinals in 2018, Hicks has been the hardest-throwing pitcher in baseball. As a rookie, he tied Aroldis Chapman's record for the fastest pitch ever thrown—105.1 mph (169 kph)!

Flamethrowers can't throw every fastball over 100 mph (161 kph). But some come close. The average speed of Noah Syndergaard's fastball is 97.6 mph (157 kph).

Some wonder if Jordan Hicks will be the first pitcher to toss a 106 mph fastball.

2019 Average Fastball Speed

RANK	PITCHER	TEAM	AVERAGE FASTBALL SPEED
1	Noah Syndergaard	New York Mets	97.6 mph (157.1 kph)
2	Gerrit Cole	New York Yankees	97.1 mph (156.3 kph)
3	Jacob deGrom	New York Mets	96.9 mph (155.9 kph)
4	Zach Wheeler	Philadelphia Phillies	96.7 mph (155.6 kph)
5	Luis Castillo	Cincinnati Reds	96.4 mph (155.1 kph)

Strikeout King

If you want to strike out a major league batter, you need to do more than just throw fast. Even with an incredible fastball, a pitcher needs to have control and throw the ball to a specific spot. Good pitchers also mix up their pitches, throwing good change-ups or curveballs along with powerful fastballs.

Nolan Ryan could do all those things and more. He struck out more batters than any pitcher in history. He holds the record for the most career strikeouts (5,714).

Nolan Ryan came close to pitching an eye-popping 12 career no-hitters. But he had five games that were broken up by a hit in the ninth inning.

Most Strikeouts in a Career

RANK	PITCHER	TEAMS	YEARS PLAYED	STRIKE-OUTS
1	Nolan Ryan	New York Mets, California Angels, Houston Astros, Texas Rangers	1966–1993	5,714
2	Randy Johnson	Montreal Expos, Seattle Mariners, Houston Astros, Arizona Diamondbacks, New York Yankees, San Francisco Giants	1988–2009	4,875
3	Roger Clemens	Boston Red Sox, Toronto Blue Jays, New York Yankees, Houston Astros	1984–2007	4,672
4	Steve Carlton	St. Louis Cardinals, Philadelphia Phillies, San Francisco Giants, Chicago White Sox, Cleveland Indians, Minnesota Twins	1965–1988	4,136
5	Bert Blyleven	Minnesota Twins, Texas Rangers, Pittsburgh Pirates, Cleveland Indians	1970–1992	3,701

The Texas Rangers carried Nolan Ryan off the field to celebrate his seventh career no-hitter in 1991.

But Nolan Ryan's most amazing record may be his seven no-hit games. He earned his seventh on May 1, 1991, when he was 44 years old. Before the game, he told his manager, "I don't feel good. I feel old today." But he didn't show it. The last batter he struck out that day hadn't even been born when Ryan started playing ball!

When the game was over, even Nolan Ryan was amazed at how well he pitched. "I never had command of all three pitches [fastball, change-up, curveball] like I did tonight," he said. "This was my most overpowering no-hitter."

Most No-Hit Games

RANK	PITCHER	YEARS PLAYED	NO-HITTERS
1	Nolan Ryan	1966–1993	7
2	Sandy Koufax	1955–1966	4
3	Justin Verlander	2005–present	3*
3	Bob Feller	1936–1956	3
3	Cy Young	1890–1911	3

*Stats listed are through the 2020 season.   19

The Oldest MLB Rookie Pitcher

Nolan Ryan's career lasted an amazing 27 years until he retired at age 46. But one great pitcher didn't even start in the major leagues until he was more than 40 years old.

Satchel Paige played most of his career before Black players were allowed to join major league teams. He played in the Negro Leagues and in Latin America. In the **off-season**, he joined traveling teams that played **exhibition** games for big crowds. Many games featured teams of Black players against teams of white players.

White MLB players who played against Satchel Paige said he was the best pitcher they ever saw. By 1947, when Jackie Robinson became the first Black player in the major leagues, Paige was famous. The following season he signed with the Cleveland Indians, even though he was nearly 42 years old.

On July 15, 1948, more than 37,000 fans packed Shibe Park in Philadelphia to see Satchel Paige pitch. He came in as a reliever. He needed only 12 pitches to strike out the side. He fanned three more batters in the next inning. The rest of that season, huge crowds turned out everywhere Paige played. Later that year, he became the first Black pitcher to play in the World Series. Baseball's oldest rookie won baseball's championship in his first year.

Oldest player in MLB history
Satchel Paige, MLB Career: 1948–53, 1965
Last game played: September 25, 1965
Age: 59

Youngest player in MLB history
Joe Nuxhall, Cincinnati Reds
First game played: June 10, 1944
Age: 15

Satchel Paige was 42 years old when he made his first MLB appearance with Cleveland on July 9, 1948.

Girl Power

The best pitchers in Little League usually throw the ball 60 to 65 mph (97 to 105 kph). But Mo'ne Davis wasn't like most teenagers. When she pitched in the Little League World Series at age 13, she threw faster than 70 mph (113 kph)!

Mo'ne's team, the Taney Dragons from Philadelphia, made the Little League World Series in 2014. When Mo'ne took the mound, she became the 18th girl to ever play in the Little League World Series. She pitched a complete game, getting eight strikeouts and giving up only two hits. She set a record as the first girl in the tournament's history to pitch a win—and get a shutout.

In high school, Mo'ne was an all-around athlete. She played basketball, soccer, and softball. Her soccer and softball teams won state championships.

Legendary Strikeouts

In 1931, 17-year-old Jackie Mitchell played for the Chattanooga Lookouts, a team in the minor leagues. When the Lookouts played an exhibition game against the New York Yankees, she pitched against Babe Ruth and Lou Gehrig. She struck out both of the legendary sluggers.

In 2014 Mo'ne Davis became the first girl to pitch a shutout game in the Little League World Series.

After her big win, Mo'ne was congratulated by Mike Trout and other sports stars. She got to meet President Barack Obama and *The Tonight Show* star Jimmy Fallon. She was even featured on the cover of *Sports Illustrated* magazine—the first Little Leaguer ever. But Mo'ne wasn't excited about the attention. "All of the interviews and the autographs and people who wanted me to take pictures, it's kind of taking away the fun," she said.

Home Run Pitchers

Before becoming a hitting legend, Babe Ruth was one of the best pitchers in the big leagues. His last season as a pitcher was in 1919. That year he pitched in 17 games while also hitting 29 home runs.

It took 99 years for another player to finally match the Babe. In 2018 Shohei Ohtani joined the Los Angeles Angels after playing five seasons in Japan. He was one of the best pitchers in his home country—and one of the best hitters.

Shohei Ohtani became the first player since Babe Ruth to pitch at least 10 games and hit more than 20 home runs in the same season.

Ohtani won his first game pitching for the Angels on April 1, 2018. Two days later, he hit his first MLB home run. The next day, he hit another. Then two days after that, he hit a third homer. Ohtani finished his first MLB season with 22 home runs batting as a designated hitter. He also pitched in 10 games that year.

The fastest pitch Shohei Ohtani ever threw went 102.5 mph (165 kph). His fastest exit velocity as a batter was 115.1 mph (185 kph).

Babe Ruth hit a record 60 home runs in a season in 1927. That mark lasted for 34 years until Roger Maris broke it in 1961. Ruth's record of 714 career home runs lasted 39 years until Hank Aaron broke it in 1974.

Chapter Three

BIG-TIME FIELDERS

The Best Defender

How do you measure a player's defensive skills? What records can a shortstop or outfielder set when they're playing in the field?

Since 2003, baseball experts have used a statistic called Defensive Runs Saved (DRS) to measure a fielder's effectiveness. DRS uses a complex formula to figure out a player's rating. Basically, it shows how many runs a fielder prevents opposing teams from scoring. A player with a DRS of 0 is an average fielder. If a player has a DRS below zero, it means he's giving up runs and playing bad defense.

Fastest Throws by Outfielders

RANK	PLAYER	TEAM	DATE	SPEED
1	Aaron Hicks	New York Yankees	4/20/16	105.5 mph (169.8 kph)
2	Brett Phillips	Milwaukee Brewers	9/19/17	104.7 mph (168.5 kph)
3	Jackie Bradley, Jr.	Boston Red Sox	6/20/18	103.4 mph (166.4 kph)
4	Carlos Gomez	Houston Astros	9/4/15	103.1 mph (165.9 kph)
5	Aristides Aquino	Cincinnati Reds	8/8/19	101.5 mph (163.3 kph)
5	Bradley Zimmer	Cleveland Indians	6/8/17	101.5 mph (163.3 kph)

The best fielders have a DRS of 10 to 15. Los Angeles Angels shortstop Andrelton Simmons has the all-time DRS record. In 2017 he finished the season with a best-ever DRS rating of 40. He bested the previous mark of 38 set in 2015 by Tampa Bay Rays centerfielder Kevin Kiermaier.

Kiermaier once told a reporter what makes a great outfielder: "If I wanted to make a darn-near-perfect outfielder, I want someone who can run, who has arm strength, accuracy, . . . great first step, all that."

Andrelton Simmons forced an out at second base during a game against the Detroit Tigers in 2018.

Highest Defensive Runs Saved Rating, Season

RANK	PLAYER	TEAM	SEASON	DRS RATING
1	Andrelton Simmons	Los Angeles Angels	2017	40
2	Kevin Kiermaier	Tampa Bay Rays	2015	38
3	Adam Everett	Houston Astros	2006	34
3	Matt Chapman	Oakland Athletics	2019	34
5	Franklin Gutierrez	Seattle Mariners	2009	33

Most Decorated Fielders

Each year both the American League and the National League honor players with the Gold Glove awards. These are given to the best player at each defensive position.

Greg Maddux holds the record for the most Gold Glove awards. He was named the best-fielding pitcher in the NL 18 times. Nearly all of the players who have won the most Gold Gloves at each position are in the Baseball Hall of Fame.

Since 2011, fans have been able to vote for baseball's best fielder in each league. After each season, fans choose from the 18 Gold Glove winners from the AL and NL. Their votes determine which players win the prized Platinum Glove awards.

Greg Maddux

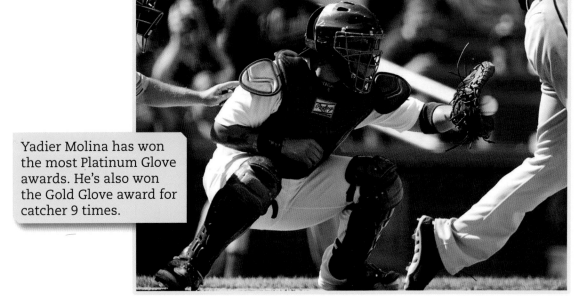

Yadier Molina has won the most Platinum Glove awards. He's also won the Gold Glove award for catcher 9 times.

Most Gold Glove Awards by Position

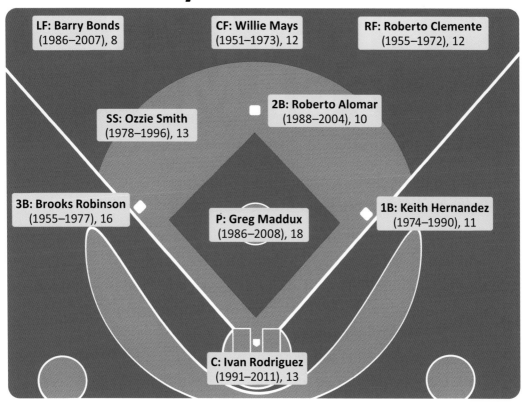

LF: Barry Bonds (1986–2007), 8

CF: Willie Mays (1951–1973), 12

RF: Roberto Clemente (1955–1972), 12

2B: Roberto Alomar (1988–2004), 10

SS: Ozzie Smith (1978–1996), 13

3B: Brooks Robinson (1955–1977), 16

P: Greg Maddux (1986–2008), 18

1B: Keith Hernandez (1974–1990), 11

C: Ivan Rodriguez (1991–2011), 13

Platinum Glove Award Winners

YEAR	NATIONAL LEAGUE	AMERICAN LEAGUE
2011	Yadier Molina, C, Cardinals	Adrián Beltré, 3B, Rangers
2012	Yadier Molina, C, Cardinals	Adrián Beltré, 3B, Rangers
2013	Andrelton Simmons, SS, Braves	Manny Machado, 3B, Orioles
2014	Yadier Molina, C, Cardinals	Alex Gordon, LF, Royals
2015	Yadier Molina, C, Cardinals	Kevin Kiermaier, CF, Rays
2016	Anthony Rizzo, 1B, Cubs	Francisco Lindor, SS, Cleveland
2017	Nolan Arenado, 3B, Rockies	Byron Buxton, CF, Twins
2018	Nolan Arenado, 3B, Rockies	Matt Chapman, 3B, Athletics
2019	Nolan Arenado, 3B, Rockies	Matt Chapman, 3B, Athletics
2020	Nolan Arenado, 3B, Rockies	Alex Gordon, LF, Royals

Chapter Four

BIG-TIME TEAMS

Baseball's Winningest Team

If you ask baseball fans which team has the most wins in history, most will probably say the New York Yankees. But the Yankees have only been around since 1903. There are seven other teams with more all-time wins than the Yankees. They were winning games long before the Yankees even existed.

The Giants are the team with the most wins in baseball history. The Giants started playing in New York City in 1883. The New York Giants were usually one of the best teams in the NL, and they won the World Series 5 times. Then in 1957, the Giants' owner moved the team to California to become the San Francisco Giants.

Buster Posey helped the Giants win the World Series in 2010, 2012, and 2014. He was NL Rookie of the Year in 2010 and MVP in 2012.

Willie Mays earned 12 Gold Glove awards and played in an incredible 24 MLB All-Star Games.

The Giants have had some of the best players in baseball history. One of these was Willie Mays, who played six seasons with the team in New York and 15 in San Francisco. When baseball fans talk about the greatest player of all time, Willie Mays is often at the top of their list.

Legendary player Willie Mays hit an amazing 660 home runs during his long career.

Most Team Wins*

RANK	NATIONAL LEAGUE	AMERICAN LEAGUE
1	Giants: 11,194	Yankees: 10,411
2	Dodgers: 11,017	Red Sox: 9,626
3	Cubs: 11,016	Cleveland: 9,512
4	Cardinals: 10,948	Tigers: 9,369
5	Braves: 10,732	White Sox: 9,318

*Stats listed are through the 2020 season.

A Record-Breaking Streak

No MLB team has ever had an undefeated season. Such a feat seems impossible with teams playing 162 regular season games. Even the greatest teams have games when their best hitters strike out, their best fielders drop the ball, or their best pitchers can't throw strikes. That's part of what makes baseball fun to watch.

But sometimes teams put everything together for a great winning streak. Everything went right for the Cleveland Indians in 2017. The team won 22 games in a row that year. They outscored other teams by a total of 142–37 during that stretch. The Indians won 13 of those games by four runs or more, and seven games were shutouts. Perhaps most amazing of all was how Cleveland trailed in only eight out of 199 innings during their streak.

But nothing lasts forever. Cleveland's streak eventually came to an end. When the team lost its first game in three weeks, more than 34,000 fans gave their team a **standing ovation.** The players came out of the dugout and tipped their hats. The Indians had won the most **consecutive** games by an AL team and the second-most in baseball history.

Most Consecutive Wins, NL (since 1901)

RANK	TEAM	YEAR	WINS
1	New York Giants	1916	26 games
2	Chicago Cubs	1935	21 games
3	New York Giants	1904	18 games
4	New York Giants	1907	17 games
4	New York Giants	1916	17 games

Most Consecutive Wins, AL

RANK	TEAM	YEAR	WINS
1	Cleveland Indians	2017	22 games
2	Oakland Athletics	2002	20 games
3	Chicago White Sox	1906	19 games
3	New York Yankees	1947	19 games
5	New York Yankees	1953	18 games

Shortstop Francisco Lindor led the Indians with nine home runs during Cleveland's winning streak.

During Cleveland's winning streak, one of their biggest fans, LeBron James, sent a message: "I've had my own 27-game winning streak in the NBA before. It's a lot of pressure winning every night."

Racking Up Player Awards

Each year after the World Series, the MLB hands out awards to its best players. The most notable awards are Rookie of the Year, the Cy Young Award for best pitcher, and the Most Valuable Player award.

If we add up the individual player awards for each team in baseball, the Dodgers come out on top. The team has racked up 44 player awards over the years. Like the Giants, the Dodgers once played in New York City, in the borough of Brooklyn. The team moved to California in 1957 along with the Giants.

After winning Rookie of the Year honors in 2017, Cody Bellinger was NL MVP in 2019.

Clayton Kershaw has won the Cy Young Award three times—in 2011, 2013, and 2014.

The Dodgers had several award-winning players when they were in Brooklyn. In 1947 Jackie Robinson was the very first player ever to be named Rookie of the Year. Today the award is named in his honor. Robinson was later named MVP in 1949. There have been five seasons when members of the Los Angeles Dodgers won both the Cy Young and MVP awards. In two of those seasons, the same player won both awards—Sandy Koufax in 1963 and Clayton Kershaw in 2014.

Teams with Most Player Awards

RANK	TEAM	ROOKIE OF THE YEAR	CY YOUNG AWARD	MVP	TOTAL
1	Dodgers	18	12	14	44
2	Yankees	9	5	22	36
3	Cardinals	6	3	20	29
4	Athletics	8	5	13	26
5	Red Sox	6	7	12	25

Record-Setting Stadiums

Baseball infields have to follow strict rules. Bases must be 90 feet (27.4 meters) apart. Home plate must be 60 feet, 6 inches (18.4 m) from the pitcher's mound. But rules about the outfield are more flexible. Ballparks can design outfield fences however they wish, as long as they meet minimum distances. Comerica Park in Detroit, Michigan, has baseball's longest centerfield. The fence is a distant 420 feet (128 m) from home plate.

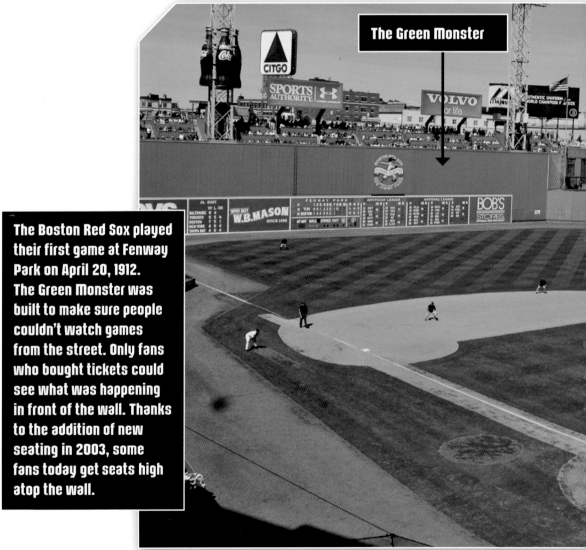

The Green Monster

The Boston Red Sox played their first game at Fenway Park on April 20, 1912. The Green Monster was built to make sure people couldn't watch games from the street. Only fans who bought tickets could see what was happening in front of the wall. Thanks to the addition of new seating in 2003, some fans today get seats high atop the wall.

Beyond the field, baseball stadiums come in various shapes and sizes. The biggest ballpark in the league is Dodger Stadium in Los Angeles, California. It can hold up to 56,000 fans. Many ballparks have unique features. One of the most famous features is at the league's oldest stadium. It's a 37-foot- (11-m-) high wall known as the Green Monster at Fenway Park in Boston, Massachusetts. It's the tallest outfield wall in the league.

BIG-TIME WORLD SERIES AND PLAYOFFS

Yankee Domination

Fans can't talk about World Series records without including the Yankees. The New York Yankees have won the most World Series championships in baseball history. They've also won more titles than any team in professional sports.

Sometimes a team wins several titles within a few seasons with the same group of players. These teams are known as **dynasties**. The Yankees have had four great dynasties. The first starred the legendary Babe Ruth and Lou Gehrig. From 1920 to 1939, they led the Yankees to play in 11 World Series and won eight titles. The last Yankees dynasty lasted from 1996 to 2000. This team won four World Series championships in those five years.

The greatest Yankee dynasty was also the most dominant team in baseball history. In the 18 seasons from 1947 to 1964, the Yankees went to the World Series an astounding 15 times and won 10 championships. They even won five World Series in a row to set the record for most consecutive titles.

MOST WORLD SERIES TITLES	
Yankees, 27	
Cardinals, 11	
Red Sox, 9	
Athletics, 9	

MOST WORLD SERIES LOSSES	
Dodgers, 14	
Yankees, 13	
Giants, 12	

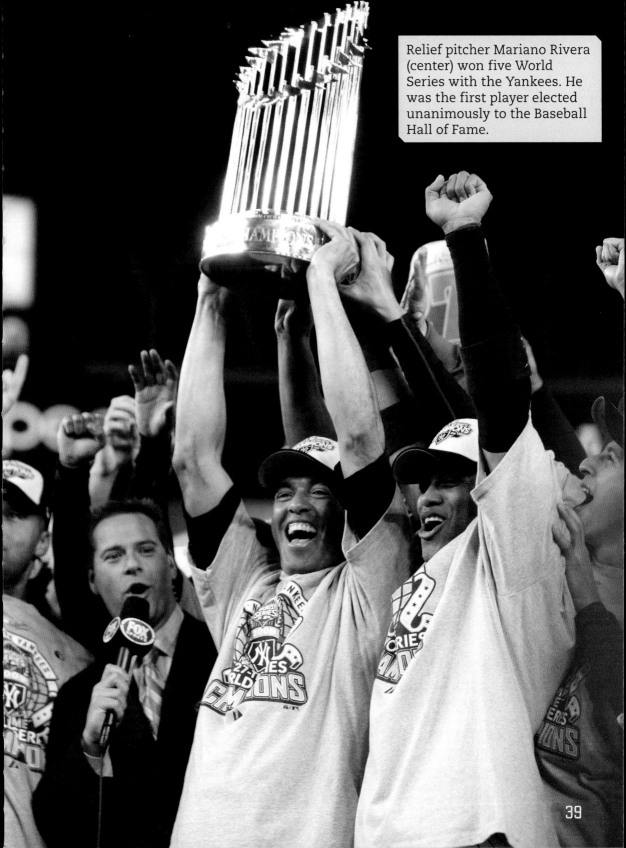

Relief pitcher Mariano Rivera (center) won five World Series with the Yankees. He was the first player elected unanimously to the Baseball Hall of Fame.

The Long Wait Ends

Serious baseball drama unfolded in Game 7 of the 2016 World Series between the Cleveland Indians and the Chicago Cubs. It was the bottom of the tenth inning, and two outs were on the board. Cleveland was down by one run, with a runner on first. The Indians had already evened up the score earlier in the game. Thousands of Indians fans were on their feet, hoping for another hit to tie the game again.

Across the country, 40 million baseball fans watched the game at home. Whatever happened, history would be made that night. Some fans wanted to see Cleveland win. It would be the Indians' first World Series title in 68 years. But many more fans were rooting for Chicago. The Cubs had gone even longer without winning a championship—107 years!

Cleveland batter Michael Martinez swung at the pitch and smacked the ball. But it bounced to Cubs third baseman Kris Bryant, who threw to first for the final out. For the first time in more than one hundred years the Cubs were World Series champions. While the team celebrated on the field, back in Chicago thousands of Cubs fans celebrated in the streets. Baseball's longest championship **drought** was finally over.

Longest Wait Between World Series Titles

107 SEASONS Chicago Cubs, 1908 to 2016

87 SEASONS Chicago White Sox, 1917 to 2005

86 SEASONS Boston Red Sox, 1918 to 2004

Chicago Cubs players and fans were ecstatic about winning their first World Series title in more than 100 years.

Longest Wait for a World Series Title

72 SEASONS
Cleveland Indians, 2 titles, last won in 1948

59 SEASONS
Texas Rangers, 0 titles, team started in 1961

51 SEASONS
Milwaukee Brewers, 0 titles, team started in 1969

51 SEASONS
San Diego Padres, 0 titles, team started in 1969

43 SEASONS
Seattle Mariners, 0 titles, team started in 1977

Breaking the Curse

Red Sox fans know how Cubs fans felt after breaking their long dry spell. In 2004, Boston had gone 86 years without winning a title. And it looked like their **curse** wasn't going to end. In the 2004 American League Championship Series, the Red Sox faced the Yankees, their biggest rivals. New York had crushed Boston 19–8 in Game 3 and needed just one more win to go to the World Series. Boston needed to win four games in a row, something no MLB team had ever done in the playoffs. But something magical was about to happen.

It looked like it was all over in the bottom of the ninth inning in Game 4. The Yankees had a 4–3 lead and Mariano Rivera, their star closer, was on the mound. But the Red Sox rallied to score the tying run and sent the game to extra innings. Then in the bottom of the twelfth inning, Boston's star slugger, David Ortiz, hit a walk-off home run to win the game.

Cursed!

When teams go a long time without winning a championship, fans often say that their team is cursed. Red Sox fans believed their team suffered from the Curse of the Bambino. It was thought Boston would never win another title after superstar Babe Ruth was sold to the rival Yankees. Cubs fans thought the Curse of the Billy Goat kept their team down. It was believed that the curse was placed on the Cubs by William Sianis, who was told to leave Wrigley Field when he brought his pet goat to a game.

Game 5 also went to extra innings and lasted almost six hours. But once again, David Ortiz was the hero, knocking in the winning run with a single. The Red Sox were still alive.

The dramatic wins in Games 4 and 5 gave the Red Sox the boost they needed. The team went on to win the next two games and the ALCS. Boston became the first team to ever win a playoff series after being down three games to none. The Red Sox moved on to the World Series and beat the Cardinals in four straight games. Their long-lasting curse was finally over.

David Ortiz is known as one of the best clutch hitters in baseball history. He had 23 walk-off hits in his career, including 11 walk-off homers.

David Ortiz was the hero of the 2004 ALCS. Led by his clutch hitting, the Boston Red Sox won their first championship in more than 80 years.

Chapter Six

THE WORLD OF BASEBALL

The World Baseball Classic

Teams that win the World Series each year are usually called the world champions. But those teams are really only champions of MLB. Teams outside the United States and Canada do not play in the World Series. For a long time, baseball didn't have an actual worldwide championship like the World Cup in soccer.

That changed in 2006. The World Baseball Classic started that year as a tournament for the world's best baseball-playing nations. Teams competed from Australia, the Dominican Republic, South Korea, Venezuela, and other countries. Several MLB stars even got to play for their home countries.

Most fans expected the U.S. team to win. It included all-star players like Derek Jeter and Ken Griffey, Jr. But Team USA didn't even make it to the semi-finals. Instead, Team Japan beat Cuba to win the first World Baseball Classic championship.

Like the soccer World Cup, the World Baseball Classic is held every four years. In the first rounds, games are hosted by several different countries. But the championship round is held in a MLB stadium in the United States.

In Japan's 10-6 win over Cuba, Ichiro Suzuki had 2 hits and scored 3 runs.

World Baseball Classic Champions

YEAR	CHAMPION	RUNNER-UP
2006	Japan	Cuba
2009	Japan	South Korea
2013	Dominican Republic	Puerto Rico
2017	USA	Puerto Rico

International Appeal

Major League Baseball sometimes seems like an **international** league. It features some of the best players from around the world. In 2020, major league players came from 20 different countries. That year the Dominican Republic had the most players in the MLB with 109.

The Dominican Republic has had a long history of players in the MLB. The first Dominican players joined the New York Giants in the 1950s. The country has also produced some of baseball's all-time greats, including sluggers David Ortiz and Albert Pujols. Every MLB team has an academy in the Dominican Republic, where teenage players practice baseball and go to school. Teams hope to find talented young players that can one day join the major leagues.

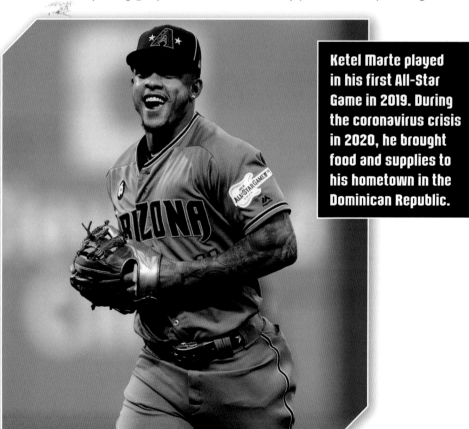

Ketel Marte played in his first All-Star Game in 2019. During the coronavirus crisis in 2020, he brought food and supplies to his hometown in the Dominican Republic.

Most International Players in MLB

COUNTRY	NUMBER OF PLAYERS, OPENING DAY 2020
Dominican Republic	109
Venezuela	75
Cuba	22
Puerto Rico	20
Mexico	9
Japan	9
Canada	9
Colombia	7
Panama	5

Teams with Most International Players

TEAM	NUMBER OF PLAYERS, OPENING DAY 2020
Twins	15
Astros	15
White Sox	13
Marlins	13
Yankees	13

Chapter Seven

LEGENDARY RECORDS, LEGENDARY PLAYERS

Baseball's Greatest Runner

The goal in baseball is simple—score more runs than the other team. To do so, teams often have the player with the best chance to score up to bat first. The team's lead-off hitter should be the best at getting to first base and the best at getting around to score.

The greatest scorer in baseball history was Rickey Henderson. In most of his 25 seasons, he got to first base in more than four out of ten at-bats. And once there, Henderson became a sneaky base runner. In his third full season, he stole 130 bases, breaking the record for most stolen bases in a season. Henderson also has the most stolen bases in a career with 1,406.

Using his base-stealing skills and speed, Rickey Henderson got around the diamond more than anyone in baseball history. In his final season, he set the record for most runs scored in a career.

Rickey Henderson could also hit with power. He holds the record for most lead-off homers with 81.

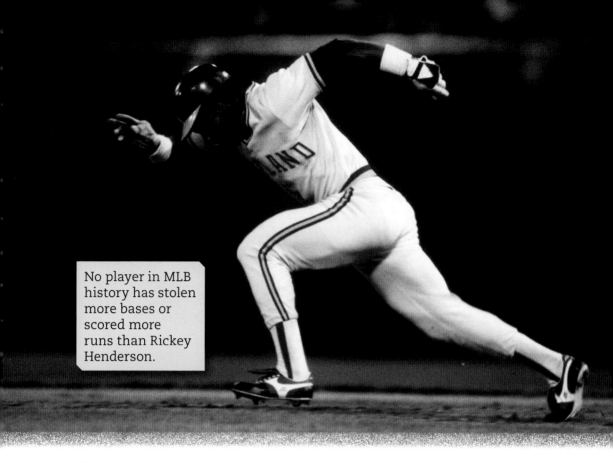

No player in MLB history has stolen more bases or scored more runs than Rickey Henderson.

Most Total Runs Scored, Career

RANK	PLAYER	YEARS PLAYED	TEAMS	RUNS SCORED
1	Rickey Henderson	1979–2003	Oakland Athletics, New York Yankees, Toronto Blue Jays, San Diego Padres, Anaheim Angels, New York Mets, Seattle Mariners, Boston Red Sox, Los Angeles Dodgers	2,295
2	Ty Cobb	1905–1928	Detroit Tigers, Philadelphia Athletics	2,245
3	Barry Bonds	1986–2007	Pittsburgh Pirates, San Francisco Giants	2,227
4	Hank Aaron	1954–1976	Atlanta Braves, Milwaukee Brewers	2,174
4	Babe Ruth	1914–1935	Boston Red Sox, New York Yankees, Atlanta Braves	2,174

Baseball's Greatest Pitcher

The **annual** award for baseball's best pitchers is named for the greatest pitcher in history.

Cy Young's real first name was Denton. He was known for throwing a wicked fastball. In a tryout, he threw pitches against a fence so hard that the wooden boards broke. People said the fence looked like it had been hit by a cyclone. They gave Young the nickname "Cyclone," which was later shortened to Cy.

Cy Young

Most Career Wins

RANK	PITCHER	YEARS PLAYED	TEAMS	WINS
1	Cy Young	1890–1911	Cleveland Spiders, St. Louis Cardinals, Boston Red Sox, Cleveland Indians, Toronto Blue Jays, Atlanta Braves	511
2	Walter Johnson	1907–1927	Washington Senators	417
3	Pete Alexander	1911–1930	Philadelphia Phillies, Chicago Cubs, Toronto Blue Jays, St. Louis Cardinals	373
3	Christy Mathewson	1900–1916	New York Giants, Toronto Blue Jays, Cincinnati Reds	373
5	Pud Galvin	1875–1892	St. Louis Brown Stockings, Buffalo Bisons, Toronto Blue Jays, Pittsburgh Pirates, Pittsburgh Burghers, St. Louis Cardinals	365

Cy Young started playing in 1890 when teams had only two or three starting pitchers. Back then pitchers usually played through entire games. Even at the end of his career, Young was pitching complete games. By the time he retired, Young had pitched an astounding 749 complete games. It's a record that will likely never be broken.

In his 22-year career, Cy Young won more games than any pitcher in MLB history. But by playing so much, he set another record too. He also lost more games than any other pitcher.

Jacob deGrom won the NL Cy Young Award in 2018 and 2019. In the first six years of his career, he won an average of 11 games each season. At that pace, he would have to play 47 years to break Cy Young's record. Cy Young got all his wins in 21 seasons.

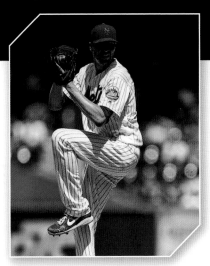

Most Career Losses

RANK	PITCHER	YEARS PLAYED	TEAMS	LOSSES
1	Cy Young	1890–1911	Cleveland Spiders, St. Louis Cardinals, Boston Red Sox, Cleveland Indians, Toronto Blue Jays, Atlanta Braves	316
2	Pud Galvin	1875–1892	St. Louis Brown Stockings, Buffalo Bisons, Toronto Blue Jays, Pittsburgh Pirates, Pittsburgh Burghers, St. Louis Cardinals	310
3	Nolan Ryan	1966–1993	New York Mets, California Angels, Houston Astros, Texas Rangers	292
4	Walter Johnson	1907–1927	Washington Senators	279
5	Phil Niekro	1964–1987	Atlanta Braves, New York Yankees, Cleveland Indians, Toronto Blue Jays	274

Baseball's Iron Man

On September 20, 1998, fans at Baltimore's Camden Yards saw one of baseball's greatest records—before the game even started. For the first time in more than 16 years, Cal Ripken, Jr. was not in the Orioles' lineup.

MLB has a long season. From April to October, teams play 162 games. With so many games, it's not unusual for players to get injured. Most players sit out games when they get hurt. But Cal Ripken, Jr. didn't. In one game he badly twisted his knee. He was back the next day. In another game he broke his nose. He was in the lineup for the next game. Fans called him "The Iron Man."

Strangely, Cal Ripken, Jr. didn't have an injury that September night in 1998. After playing 2,632 consecutive games, Baltimore's star had just decided it was time to take a break. When the other team saw Ripken sitting on the bench, they stepped out of the dugout and clapped. The fans rose to their feet and cheered, realizing they had just seen a record that may never be broken.

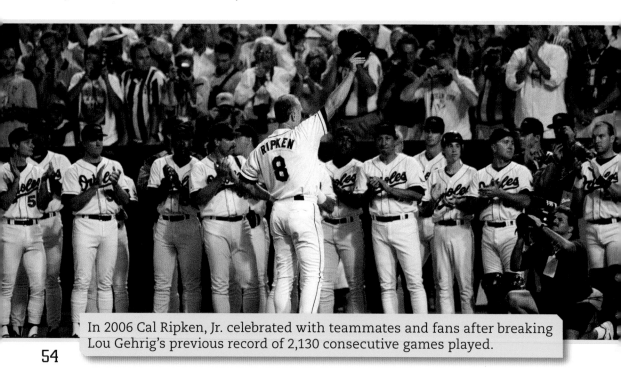

In 2006 Cal Ripken, Jr. celebrated with teammates and fans after breaking Lou Gehrig's previous record of 2,130 consecutive games played.

For five seasons, Cal Ripken, Jr. played every inning of every game. He set a record of 8,243 consecutive innings.

Most Consecutive Games Played

RANK	PLAYER	CONSECUTIVE GAMES	YEARS OF STREAK	TEAMS
1	Cal Ripken, Jr.	2,632	1982–1998	Baltimore Orioles
2	Lou Gehrig	2,130	1925–1939	New York Yankees
3	Everett Scott	1,307	1916–1925	Boston Red Sox, New York Yankees, Washington Senators
4	Steve Garvey	1,207	1975–1983	Los Angeles Dodgers, San Diego Padres
5	Miguel Tejada	1,152	2000–2007	Oakland Athletics, Baltimore Orioles

Lou's Number

Before Ripken, Lou Gehrig was baseball's Iron Man. He had played for 17 years and set the record of 2,130 consecutive games. But he ended his career in 1939. Doctors had discovered that Gehrig had a disease called ALS. The disease causes victims to grow weak and lose control of their bodies. The Yankees honored him by retiring his jersey number. No other Yankee player would ever wear number 4 again. Lou Gehrig was the first person in any sport to have his number retired. He died from ALS in 1941.

Honored by the Hall of Fame

The greatest honor for a player is to be elected to the Baseball Hall of Fame in Cooperstown, New York. Only the very best players are selected. Rules require that a player must be retired for at least five years before being voted into the Hall. Many players wait even longer before going to Cooperstown.

But Roberto Clemente was the exception. He was named to the Hall of Fame without the required waiting period. During his 18-year career, Clemente was one of the game's best players. He was also very popular and did a lot of **charity** work, especially on his home island of Puerto Rico. On December 31, 1972, Clemente took off in a plane to bring supplies to Nicaragua. Sadly, the plane crashed, and Clemente was killed.

Roberto Clemente was elected to the Hall of Fame just three months after his death. He was the first player from Latin America to join baseball's greats at Cooperstown. Players from Latin America are now among the very best in baseball.

The Pittsburgh Pirates retired Roberto Clemente's number 21. Latino players in MLB have also decided to retire his number across the league. No player from Latin America wears number 21, in honor of the game's greatest Latin American player.

During his career, Roberto Clemente played in 15 All-Star Games and won 12 Gold Glove awards. He won two World Series titles, a World Series MVP award, and was named the NL MVP in 1966.

The Greatest Honor

Fans may claim that several record-setting players could be called the greatest. But among all MLB teams, there is only one player who is considered the most important—Jackie Robinson.

Jackie Robinson began playing for the Brooklyn Dodgers on April 15, 1947. Before that time, Black players were banned from the major leagues. Baseball fans can only imagine how amazing it would have been to see young Satchel Paige pitch against Babe Ruth. But fans weren't allowed to see this because the white men who ran the league refused to sign Black players.

Even after Jackie Robinson broke the color barrier, there were still some who thought that Black people didn't belong in baseball. But thankfully, Jackie Robinson helped to prove that way of thinking was wrong. His professional character and great play on the field gradually changed people's opinions and attitudes toward Black people.

In 1997 the league granted Jackie Robinson a special honor that no other athlete in any other sport had ever received before. Every MLB team retired Robinson's number 42. No other player will ever wear his number again.

MLB players are only allowed to wear number 42 on April 15. The league celebrates that day each year as Jackie Robinson Day. Every player on every team wears number 42.

As a college student at UCLA, Jackie Robinson was an all-around athlete. He competed in football, basketball, track, and baseball. Baseball was actually his worst sport.

Jackie Robinson slid safely into home in Game 1 of the 1955 World Series against the New York Yankees.

MAJOR LEAGUE BASEBALL TIMELINE

1876
National League founded

1884
Charles Radbourn of the Providence Grays wins 60 games

1901
American League founded

1903
First World Series played

1911
Cy Young wins 511th game with the Boston Rustlers

1912
Fenway Park opens

1916
New York Giants win 26 straight games

1927
Babe Ruth hits 60 home runs for the New York Yankees

1939
Yankees first baseman Lou Gehrig
sits out after 2,130 straight games

1947
Jackie Robinson plays for the Brooklyn Dodgers

1953
Yankees win their fifth consecutive World Series

1958
New York Giants and Brooklyn Dodgers move to California

1973
The Pittsburgh Pirates' Roberto Clemente
is elected to the Baseball Hall of Fame

1982
Cal Ripken, Jr. begins consecutive game streak
with Baltimore Orioles

1991
Nolan Ryan pitches 7th no-hitter
with the Texas Rangers

2004
Boston Red Sox win first World Series since 1918

2006
Japan wins first World Baseball Classic

2014
Mo'ne Davis of the Taney Dragons pitches
shutout in Little League World Series

2016
Chicago Cubs win first World Series since 1908

2019
Minnesota Twins hit 307 home runs

GLOSSARY

annual (AN-yoo-uhl)—something that happens every year

charity (CHAYR-uh-tee)—a group that raises money or collects food or goods to help people in need

consecutive (kuhn-SEK-yuh-tiv)—when something happens several times in a row without a break

curse (KURS)—a long period in which a team fails to have much success; often thought to be due to something that happened in the past

drought (DROUT)—a long period of time when a player or team has little success

dynasties (DYE-nuh-stees)—teams that win multiple championships over a period of several years

exhibition (ek-suh-BI-shuhn)—a game played only for show and not part of the normal schedule; exhibition games do not count in a team's standings

international (in-tur-NASH-uh-nuhl)—including more than one nation

off-season (OFF-SEE-zuhn)—the time of year when a sport is not played

radar (RAY-dar)—an electronic device that uses radio waves to measure the speed of an object

rookie (RUK-ee)—a first-year player

scouts (SKOUTS)—people who look for players who might be able to play as professionals

standing ovation (STAN-ding oh-VAY-shuhn)—when an entire audience stands up to cheer and applaud a performance

unique (you-NEEK)—one of a kind

velocity (vuh-LOSS-uh-tee)—a measurement of both the speed and direction of a moving object

READ MORE

Chandler, Matt. *Pro Baseball Records: A Guide for Every Fan.* North Mankato, MN: Capstone Press, 2019.

Hetrick, Hans. *Baseball's Record Breakers.* North Mankato, MN: Capstone Press, 2017.

Morey, Allan. *Baseball Records.* Minneapolis, MN: Bellwether Media, Inc., 2018.

Rajczak, Michael. *The Greatest Baseball Players of All Time.* New York: Gareth Stevens Publishing, 2020.

INTERNET SITES

10 Baseball Records That Will Never Be Broken
bleacherreport.com/articles/188252-10-baseball-records-that-will-never-be-broken

Major League Baseball Facts for Kids
kids.kiddle.co/Major_League_Baseball

Overall Baseball Leaders and Baseball Records
www.baseball-reference.com/leaders/

These MLB Records Might be Unbreakable
mlb.com/news/baseball-records-that-will-never-be-broken-c281308266

INDEX